JIM HUTCHINGS

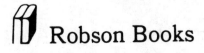
Robson Books

First published in Great Britain in 1989 by Robson Books Ltd,
Bolsover House, 5–6 Clipstone Street, London W1P 7EB

Copyright © 1989 Jim Hutchings

British Library Cataloguing in Publication Data

Hutchings, Jim
    Neighbours! : a humorous peep at them next door.
    1. English humorous cartoons–collection
    741.5'942

ISBN 0 86051 615 6

Printed and bound in Great Britain by
Biddles Ltd, Guildford and King's Lynn

Neighbourhood Watch

A survey reports here that one in three people
actually hate their neighbours — what nonsense!

Next door moved out this morning and Cyril's
really rather pleased about it.

Well, yes, I was ogling your daughter but I was
also admiring your roses.

You've probably guessed by now that you've
moved next door to a cat person.

Can I borrow your hammer?

It's extraordinary the lengths he'll go to put one
over on them.

How's reception tonight, dear?

... And what's more, the seeds from your bloody weeds are blowing straight over on to my rose beds.

She bought that thing for the Royal Wedding
and, by God, she's made good use of it since.

There's something very peculiar about the new couple next door, they keep trying to engage me in conversation.

I used to complain about it but now I wouldn't
be without it.

Well, I *am* an unsocial bugger and I want *eight* foot.

The wife said she'd like a flap on it for when they're not speaking.

... And when you see that lot next door, give 'em
an ear full of Love Thy Neighbour....

Well, I don't suppose the new neighbour likes
the look of you either, dear.

I see we've got the bluetits again this year.

That's the only time I've ever known him to
agree with anyone.

Here's looking at you, kid.

During the week, he's Something in the City.

You know you thought that our nasty neighbour
was away on holiday? Well, guess who's sitting
on next door's balcony?

I'd appreciate it, Mrs Jones, if you wouldn't
flick worms, snails and slugs over to my side
of the fence.

It's next door looking for trouble again, dear—
are you in?

Damn it Mavis, they've not only got a new car,
it's a three-litre DRL Super De Luxe Injection
bloody Special!

Well, you might call 'em *bellis perennis,* I call 'em
bleedin' daisies!

It's not a shed, dear, it's a gazebo—apparently.

I know next door don't even know we're away,
but she's damned well getting a card just the
same.

My neighbour 'ates our Thursday night practice.

No, I didn't know next door's landing light came
on after midnight and no, I don't know what it
means.

As neighbours go, he's fine but make any snide remarks about gnomes and all hell breaks loose.

Music lovers? I'll give 'em bloody music lovers!

Ignore him, dear, just ignore him.

Come off it, Mr Patterson, you haven't mislaid
anything of the kind.

I shouldn't bother to go next door, they know
everything anyway.

They've got most of the things I usually borrow
Beryl, ladder, mower, workmate, steps....

Is there any chance you could turn that radio down, stop your ruddy dogs barking, kids screaming and put a silencer on your blasted mower or, better still, *move?*

You say 'Who's a nosey ol' bugger then' once
more and I'll wring your neck.

Next door? Very nice little family, no trouble at all.

Asking the new neighbour in for a welcome
drink wasn't such a good idea after all.

I'm afraid that all the properties in your price
bracket, sir, come *with* neighbours.

Just look at that — we get a sundial and they
have to top it.

I've been next door to meet the new neighbours, dear. They're very nice, their names are John and Vera. He's a sales representative for a textile company, so I bet that car isn't his. She works as a receptionist at the local health centre, so she'll know a thing or two and they have a daughter that they're very cagey about. Pop round Harry and introduce yourself and see what you can find out.

Doctor Livingstone, I presume?

Good evening, sir. Super Double Glazing
Limited. The gentleman next door said you were
in the market.

Dad said, 'Thanks for the loan of the mower and
did you know that you can get an updated
version of it now?'

You won't be objecting to my planning
application, will you Watney?

I thought I'd get it done, they forecast rain
for tomorrow.

Strewth, he's been in next door's pond again,
dear. You can do some chips with this one.

Why would I want John Innes Number Two?
I'm burying the cat.

If the next letter isn't 'M', it ruddy well ought to be.

Your dog's got into my garden again and yes,
you can borrow my shovel *again*.

Strange thing is, I never seem to get much fruit
at *that* end.

I finally flipped and set about the neighbour this
morning.

Put a match to that lot chum and you'll never be
the same man again.

'Allo, she's sunbathing in the nude again.

That cheeky bugger next door just asked me if I
had planning permission for it.

But I'm getting 20p a bunch for them.

You ought to be pleased, it's instant death to
blackfly.

Why don't you go next door? They've got some
really nice stuff in there.

Not *Capability* Brown?

Hello, Tom Beresford on Remote here.

Bloody show off.

My dad says — when it comes to gardening,
you've a great deal to learn.

'Dear Harry—you will remember a few weeks
ago that you impressed upon me the
importance of improving the relationship with
our neighbour, well....'

Up the workers!

I reckon ol' misery next door's been talking to 'em.

Damn! I think they've noticed it.

I wanted one more along the lines of 'Get
Stuffed'.

Steady on Eric, it's only a man with a clipboard
not the actual removal van.

I could understand it for a decent-sized dog, but
a bloody hamster!

Have you got one for cleaning foul mouths?

I'm still undecided what to do, cut it off or poke
it back.

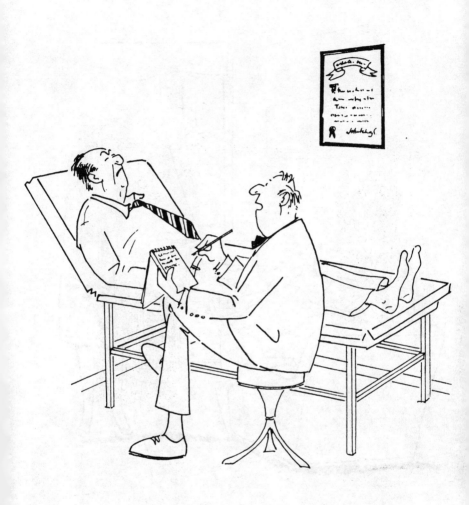

And have you always felt this aggression towards
your neighbour or has it only been since work
began on his extension?

Now next door have made it up with me, Arthur,
they're going to let us look after their animals
while they're away.

The noise of your mower's bad enough mate —
spare us the operatics!

Guess what I've found of yours in the middle of
my compost heap?

D'you mean the estate agents haven't
mentioned next door's 23-foot Julian Class
Mark 4 Caledonian sloop?

Do something outrageous Gladys, they're
peeping from their bedroom window again.

How about the key to your tool shed while
you're away?

At the moment, your mum's not speaking to my
dad but talks to my mum and your dad's not
speaking to my dad but speaks to my mum.

Throw a note over dear to say we've got the
message or he'll be parading up and down when
the Gaulton-Smiths arrive.

Quite frankly, Vicar, I wouldn't covet his wife, his
manservant, his maidservant, his ox or 'is ruddy
ass if they paid me.

The couple before you didn't object to it.
Anyway, why do you think your place is called
Rose Cottage?

They were a nice enough couple who've just
moved out but what with the wife's violin and
my euphonium....

Don't you love this time of year, Mr Harvey?

It's Mr Pratt from next door dear, he want's to
wish you a happy New Year.

Well, yes, it's true I didn't love my neighbour but
then he *was* a bit of a bastard.